Original publication: "Notopísanka 2"
Author: Eva Šašinková, M.M., Ph.D., M.B.A.
Illustrations: Mgr. Kateřina Kovářová
Original graphic design: Lumír Kaděra
Original publisher: Czech Music Edition, Prague, Czech Republic, 2023
Website: www.hudebni-publikace.cz
Copyright: Eva Šašinková, M.M., Ph.D., M.B.A.
Original Czech version ISBN: 978-80-908706-2-8

English adaptation: "Clefi's Music Workbook 2"
Illustrations: Mgr. Kateřina Kovářová
Translation, adaptation, and graphic design: Roman Placzek, D.M.A.
Publisher: BumbleBeeNotes™ Music Publishing, Manlius, NY, USA, 2024
Catalog number: cbbn002-wb-004
Website: www.bumblebeenotes.com
Copyright: BumbleBee Notes™ Inc. Music Corporation
ISBN: 979-8-9919035-3-0

What's Inside:

Note duration, pitch, and staff and keyboard placement
Measure
Notes of the fourth octave + C5
Notes of the fifth octave
Notes of the third octave in the treble clef
Substitute musical staff - the hand staff
Ascending and descending melodies
Major fifth chord

Hi, little musicians!

I must say that you are an awesome bunch! Your work with the duration of notes and rests was outstanding, and you earned your first Music Workbook Certificate! Congratulations! I have prepared a new workbook for you. In this one, we will practice reading and writing notes in the treble clef. The rhythm is like your second language by now, so we will focus on the notes' pitch. We will play, draw, write, and sing new songs. And to make it even more exciting, we will learn some new musical secrets that aren't included in my Little Notebook. It's a surprise! I am thrilled to see you soon!

Yours, Clefi

Similar to "Clefi's Little Notebook," this book presents a collection of enchanting folk songs from the rich Czech folklore tradition, designed for music education. To accurately utilize their intended purpose, each song requires accurate adaptation and translation into English, which would take up more space than these volumes can accommodate without disrupting their intended design. Therefore, we are offering a standalone "Clefi & Notelina's Songbook," featuring all the songs from all nine volumes of Clefi's New Music Education School series, along with accurately and sensibly translated and adapted English lyrics.

Welcome Review

	NOTE	REST	NUMBER OF BEATS	
WHOLE				
HALF				
QUARTER				
EIGHTH				

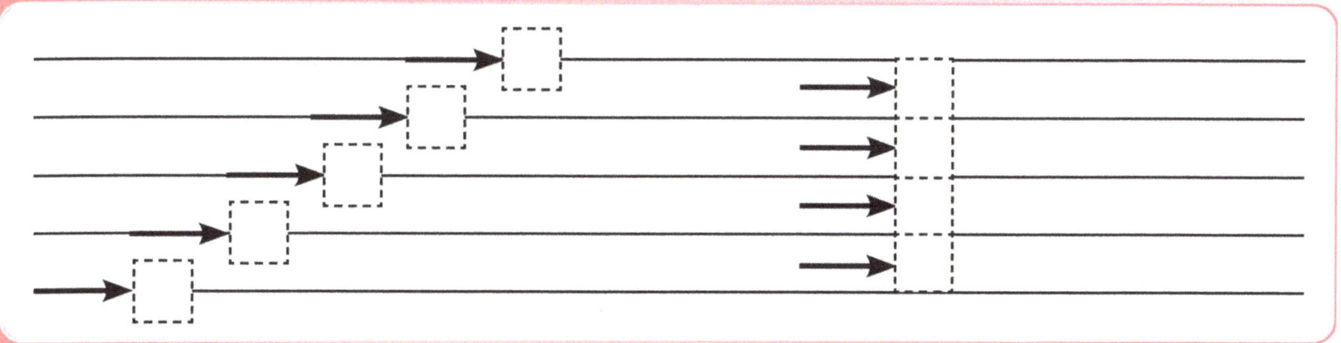

E The **musical staff** has _____ lines and _____ spaces.
Number the lines and **spaces** of the **musical staff**.

E Draw the **whole notes** according to the **placement labels** below the **measures**.

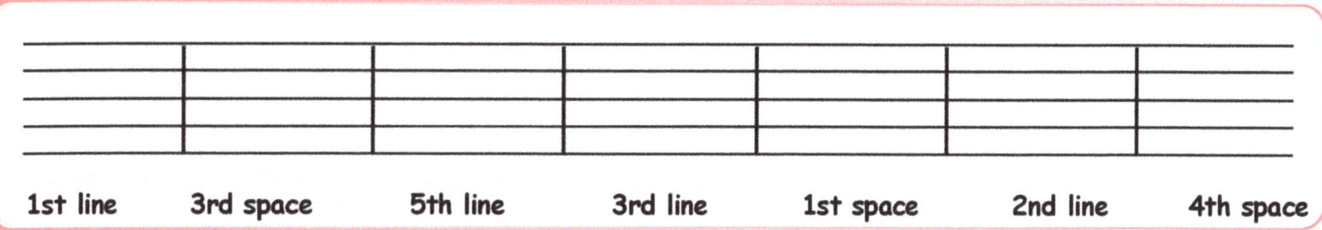

E Fill the musical staff with beautiful **treble clefs**.

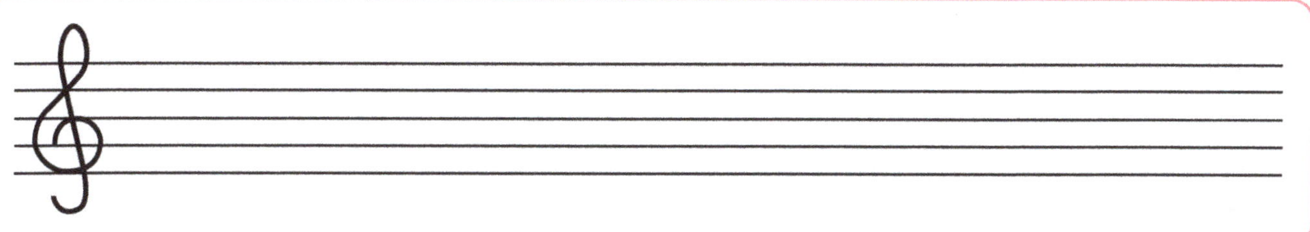

Note Duration

E Circle the **whole notes** and **rests in blue**, the **half notes** and **rests in green**, the **quarter notes** and **rests in red**, and the **eighth notes and rests in yellow**.

E Write the **note** and **rest duration** in the **number of beats** into the **empty cherries** of the pairs.

Measure

Clefi's Little Notebook, pg. 30 and 31

TWO-FOUR MEASURE has two beats 

THREE-FOUR MEASURE has three beats 

THE FOUR-FOUR MEASURE
(common)
has four beats

E Fill in the **time signatures** according to the **number of beats**.

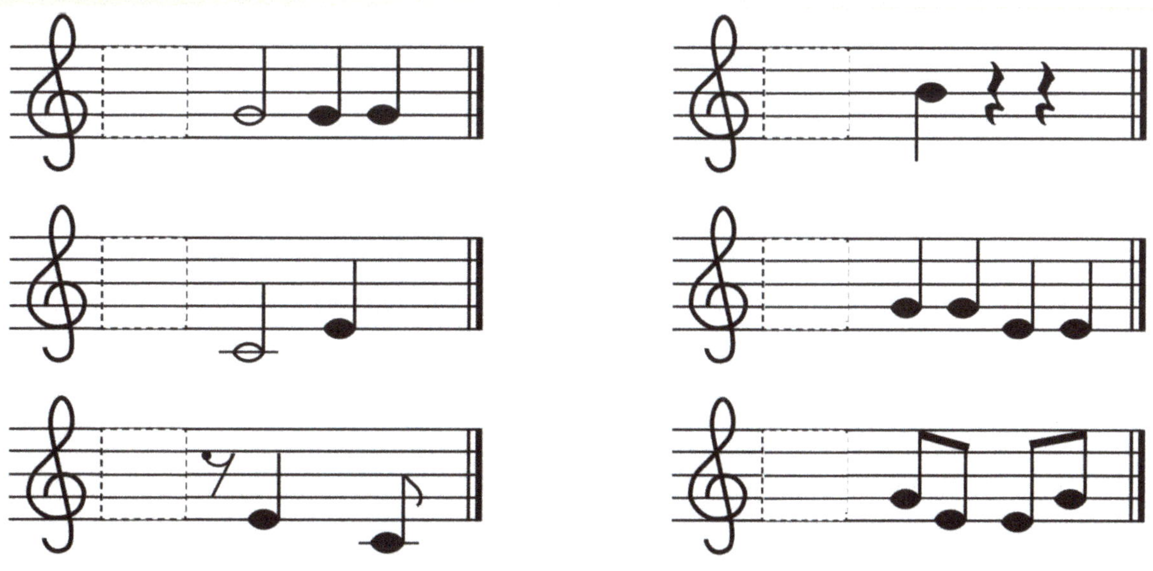

E Complete the measure with the **right notes** according to the **time signatures**.

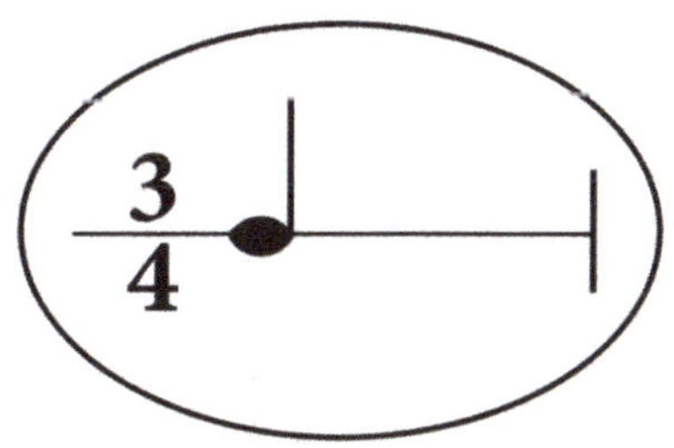

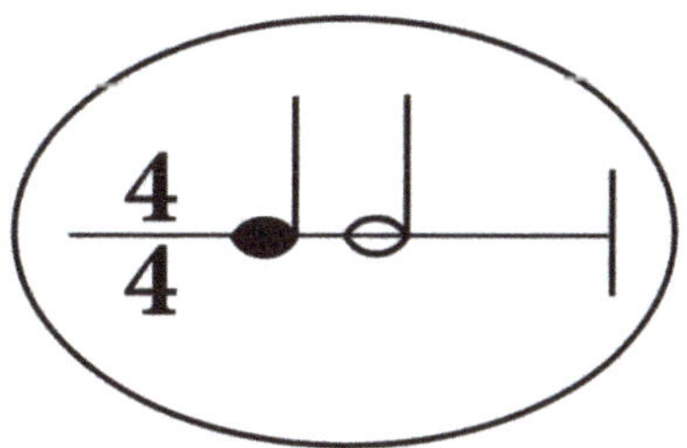

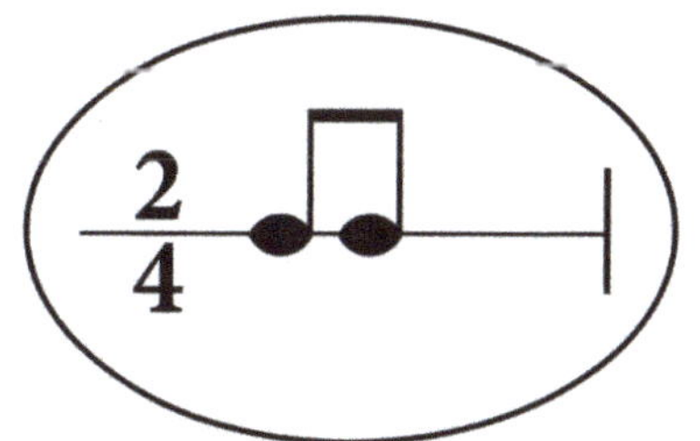

Note Pitch & Placement

The notes with **higher pitches** are placed in the **upper part** above the musical staff, with the stems on the **left side downward**.

The notes with **lower pitches** are placed in the **lower part** and **below the musical staff** with the **stems** on the **right side upward**.

E
- **Trace** the **middle line** of the **staff**.
- Circle the **notes** in the **upper part** of the staff in **red** and those in the **lower part** in **blue**.
- Read the **notes' placement** aloud, like this: *"In the treble clef, the C4 sits on the first ledger line below the staff."*

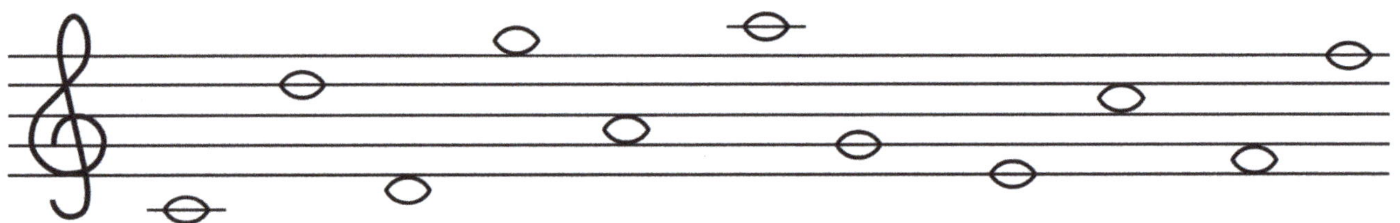

E Complete the **half notes** with correctly placed **stems**.

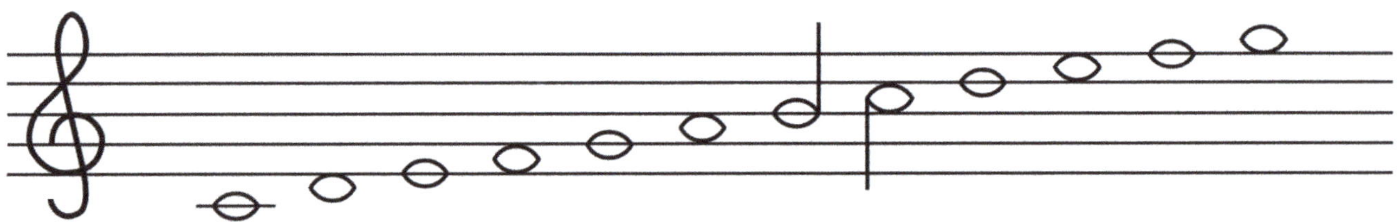

E Sing "The C Major Song" from *Clefi's Little Notebook* (pg. 38) and **memorize** the **primary tone row - the C Major scale**. Complete the **quarter notes** with correctly placed **stems**.

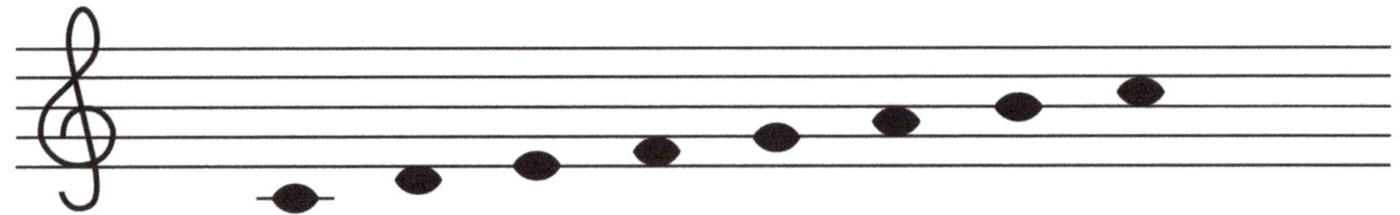

The tones of the **primary tone row** - C, D, E, F, G, A, B - are played on the **white keys** of the keyboard. The primary tones **repeat** several times at **different pitches**. We call these individual groups of the primary tones **octaves**. The **middle octave** (in the middle of the keyboard) is the **fourth octave**. To identify their specific pitches, the notes of the middle and all the other octaves carry their octaves' **numbers**:

C4, D4, E4, F4, G4, A4, B4.

E Write the **names** of the **tones** with the arrows into the **squares**.

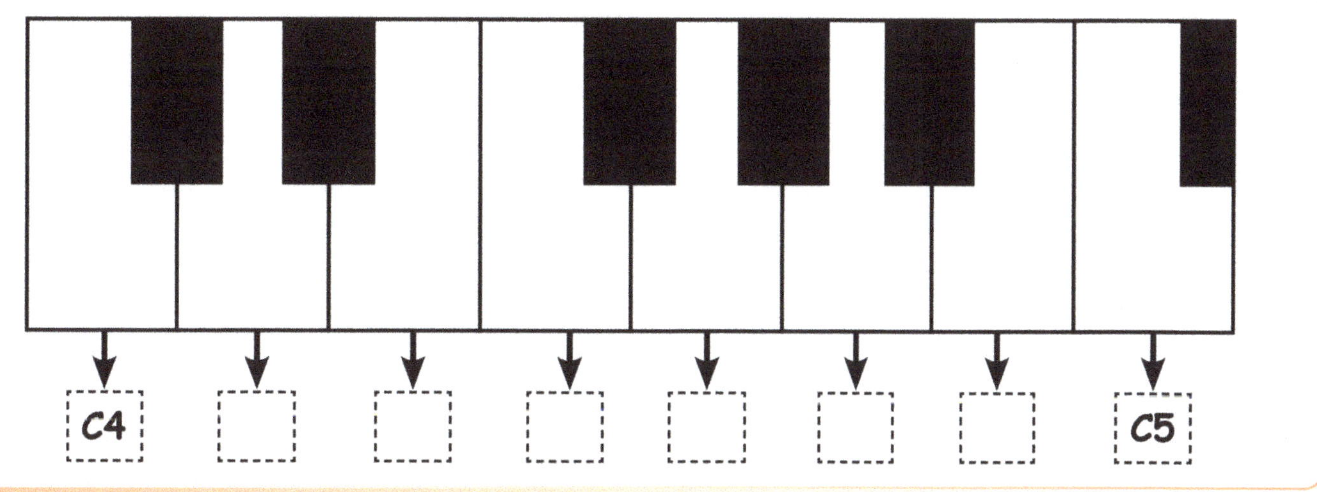

E Now, let's look at the **same tones** and the **notes** on the **musical staff** and **name** them. Circle the **notes** on a **line** in **yellow**, the **notes** in a **space** in **green**, the note **under the staff** in **red**, and the note on the **ledger line** in **blue**.

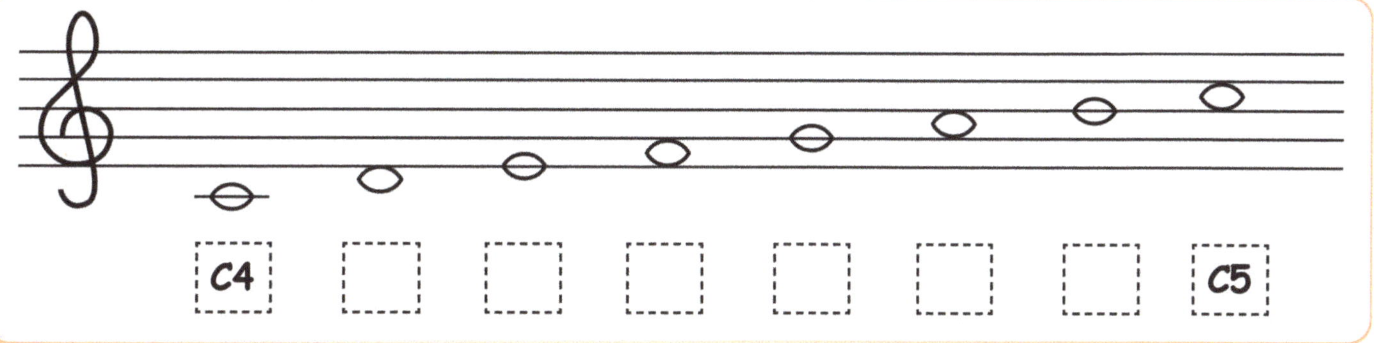

E Fill in the **missing tones** of the **tone row**. Color each **section** of the cute scale warm according to the **assignment** in the **previous exercise**.

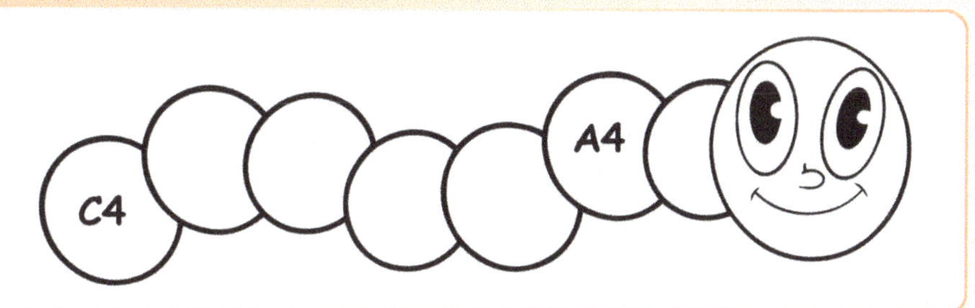

Notes C4 and D4

Clefi's Little Notebook, pg. 40 and 42

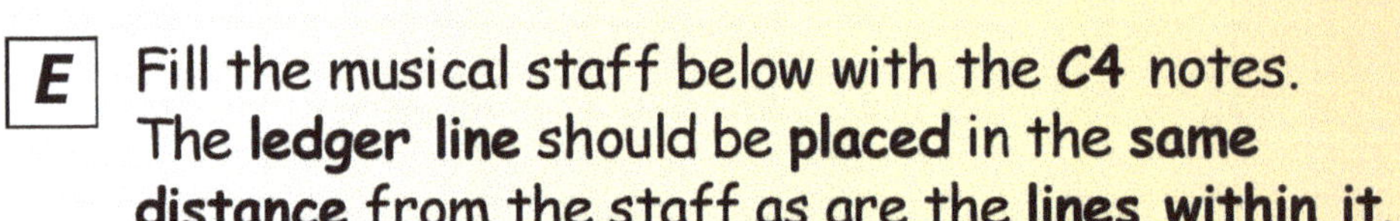

In the **treble clef**, the primary note **C4** sits on the **first ledger line under** the **staff**, like a pebble on the Covered Road in *Clefi's Little Notebook* on page 39.

E Fill the musical staff below with the **C4** notes. The **ledger line** should be **placed** in the **same distance** from the staff as are the **lines within it**.

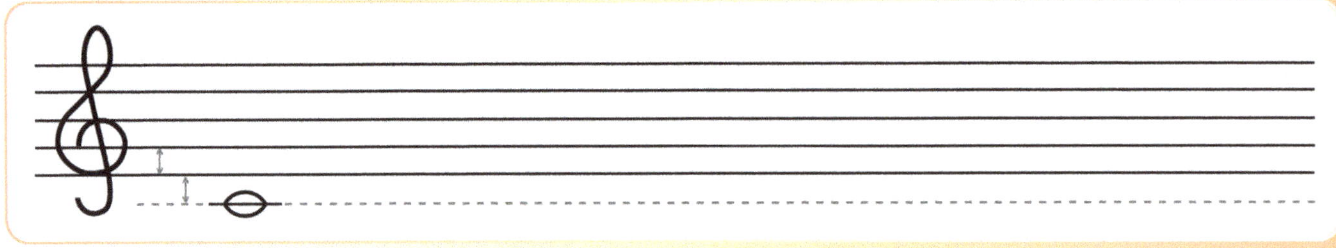

E Fill the staff with the **alternating C4 quarter** and **eighth notes**. Pay attention to the **length** of their **stems**.

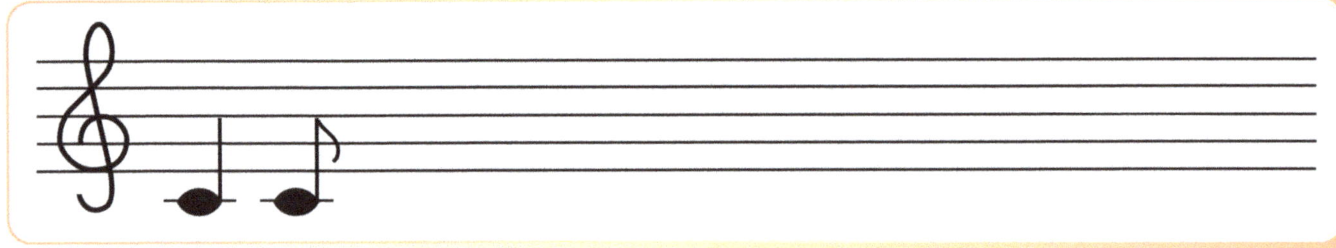

All the notes in the picture have the **same size heads** and the **same length stems**.

E Add **stems** to all **notes** and **circle** the note **C4** in **red**.

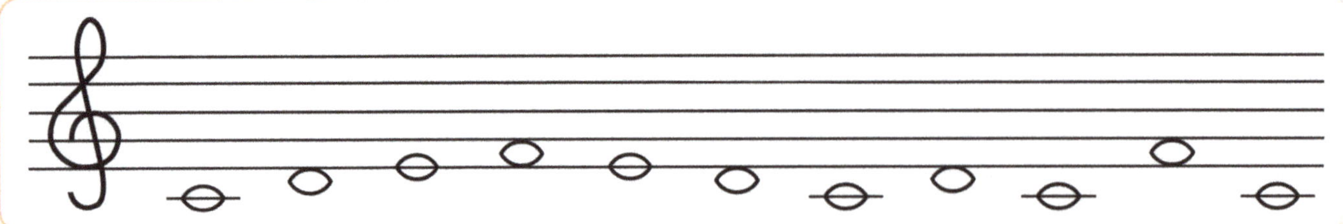

In the **treble clef**, the primary note **D4 hangs** right **below** the **first line** of the **staff**, like the house **down** the pebbles-covered road in *Clefi's Little Notebook* on page 39.

E Practice drawing the D4 **half**, **quarter**, and **eighth notes**.

E Fill the staff with the **alternating C4** and **D4 notes**. How **long** are they?

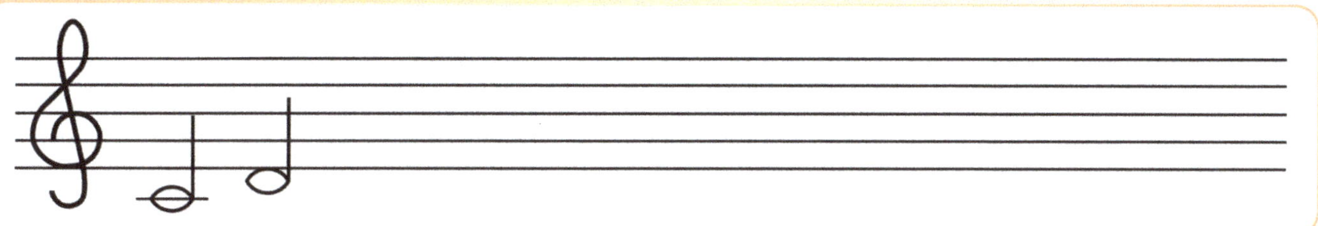

E Find the **notes** you just **learned** in the song "Cat is Coming Down." Circle the **C4** notes in **red** and the **D4** notes in **blue**.

Write out the **complete names** of all the notes on the staff.
Next, modify their durations by filling in their heads and adding stems,
ensuring you end up with **no more than four whole notes**, and **at least two
half notes, one quarter note**, and **two eighth notes.**

Find the **clouds** with **correctly written notes** and **color them blue.**

E Complete the **half notes** by adding **correctly placed stems**. Circle note **C4 red** and note **D4 green**.

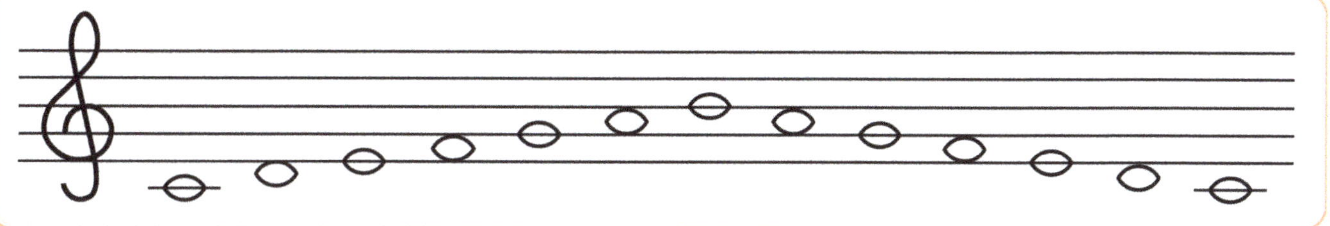

E Draw the **treble clef** at the beginning of the staff and write the **eighth notes** according to their **names** below the staff. Pay attention to the **length** and the **placement** of the **stems** and the **direction** of the **flags**.

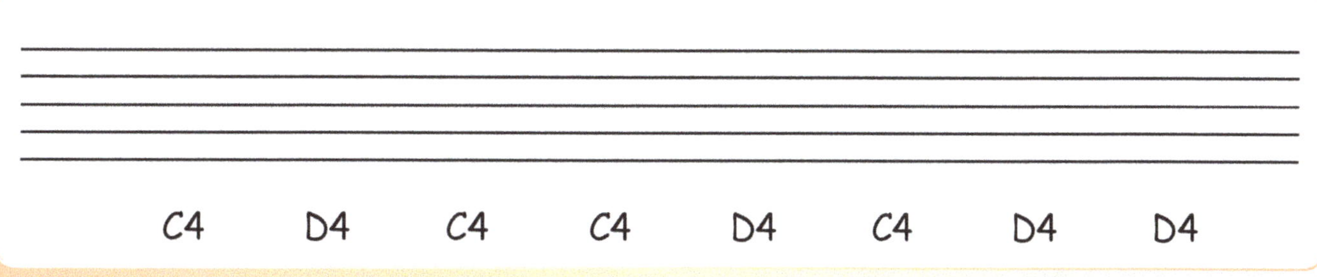

E Look at the first balloon and **complete** the remaining ones by **adding** the name of the **note above** and the **corresponding number of beats** below the lines. Then, color the balloons!

E Highlight all **incorrectly** written **notes** in red.

Note E4

In the **treble clef**, the primary note **E4** sits on the **first line** of the **staff**, like the swallow Ellen perched on the first power line in *Clefi's Little Notebook* on page 39.

E Practice drawing the **E4** half, **quarter**, and **eighth notes**.

E Learn to **recognize** the note E4. Circle all the **notes E4** you can find with **different** colors.

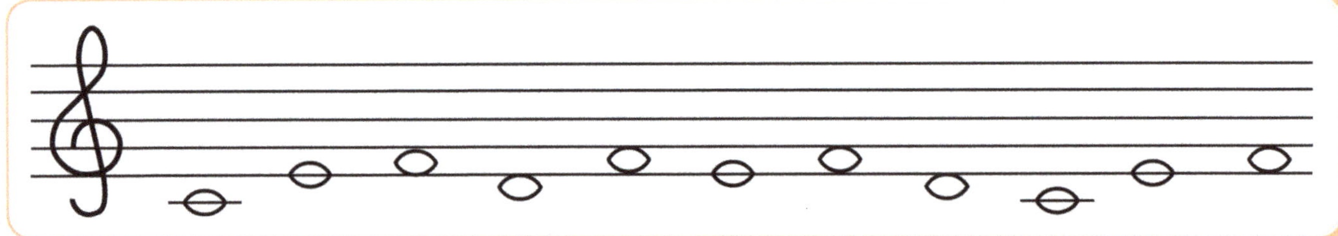

E **Notate** the beginning of the song "Go to Sleep, My Little Starlight." You can find it in *Clefi's Little Notebook* on page 52. The **dots** and **dashes** below the **names** of the **notes** indicate their **duration**.

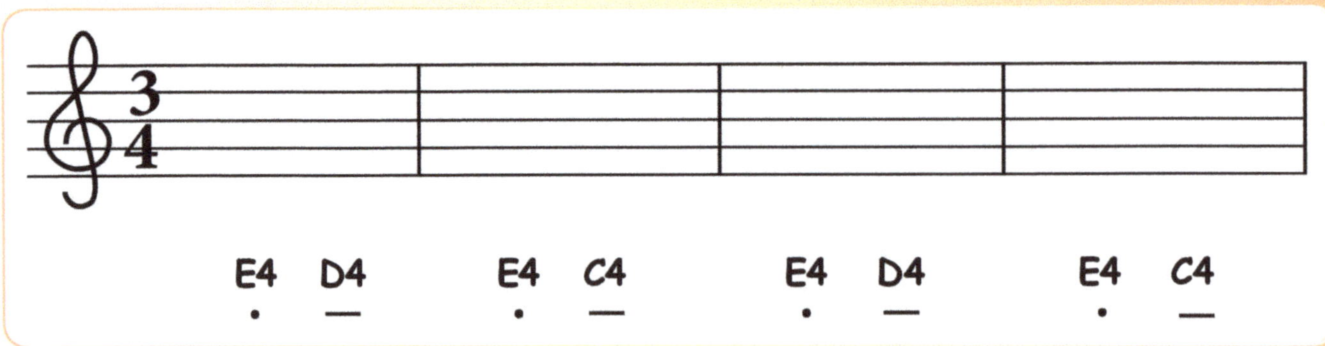

Note F4

In the **treble clef**, the primary note **F4** sits in the **first space** of the **staff**, like the little robin Frank fluttering between the first and the second lines in *Clefi's Little Notebook* on page 39.

E Practice drawing the **F4 half**, **quarter**, and **eighth notes**.

E See how many notes you know. Write the **full names** of the **notes** on the dotted line below the staff. Add **stems** to each note, then **change** three of them to **quarter** and another **four** to **eighth notes**.

E Circle the **higher note** in every **measure** in **different colors**. Write the **names** of the **notes** on the dotted line below the staff.

Learn the lovely children's song about a little sheep and her friend,
a little ram. **Sing** it while **clapping** to the **beats** and the **rhythm**.

E **Find** the **measures** from the train cars below in the **song above**, and **fill in** the measures that **come next**. Then, **arrange** the wagons in the correct **order** by **numbering** them.

E The **rhythmic notation** of the song is **incomplete**. **Add** the **missing notes**.

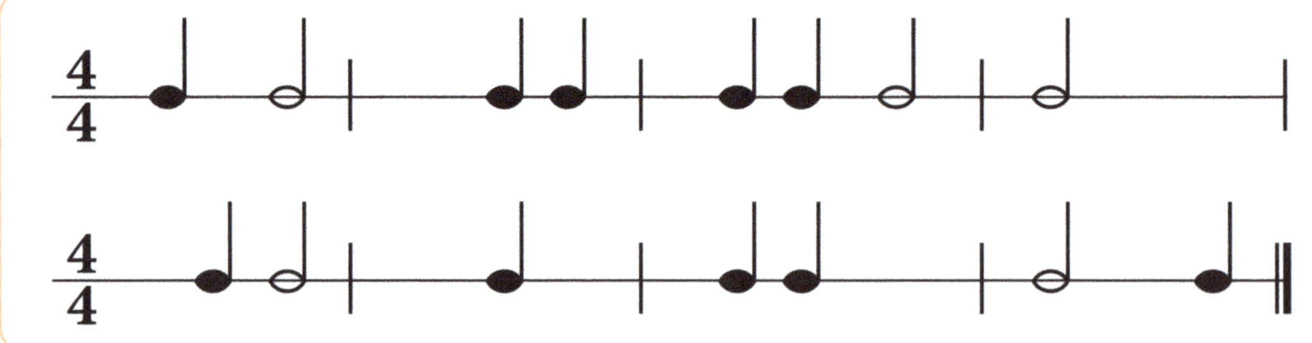

Note G4

Clefi's Little Notebook, pg. 40 and 41

In the **treble clef**, the primary note **G4** sits on the **second line** of the **staff**, like the swallow Gaby perched on the second power line in *Clefi's Little Notebook* on page 39.

E Practice drawing the **G4** half, **quarter**, and **eighth notes**.

E **Learn, sing,** and **clap** the song about a geese herding girl. Circle all **G4** notes.

E **Copy** the **measures** with the words "girl" and "curl."

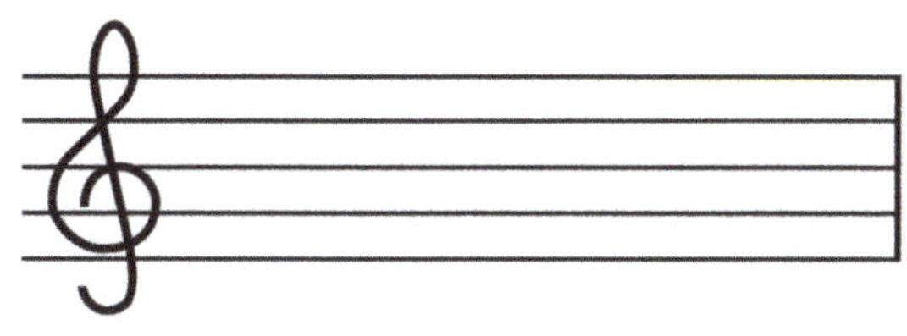

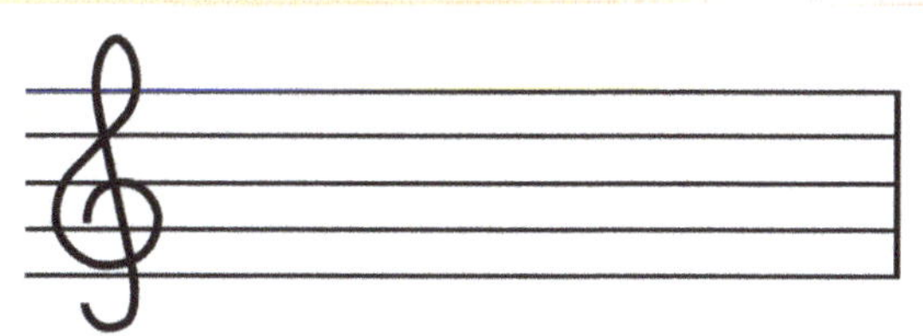

E The wind blew and scattered the measures of the song "Don't Be Mad, My Little Piggy." **Rearrange** the leaves and **write** them on the **staff** below in the **correct** order. **Sing** each measure using the **names** of the **notes**.

Clefi & Notelina's Songbook, pg. 34

E Color each section of the picture according to the "rest" color scheme:

- Use **pink** for the **sections** featuring a **quarter rest**.
- Apply **brown** to the **sections** that include an **eighth rest**.
- Color the **sections** with a **half rest** in **green**.
- Use **red** for the **sections** with a **whole rest**.

E **How many** rests did you find? Write the **numbers** in the boxes below the **rests**.

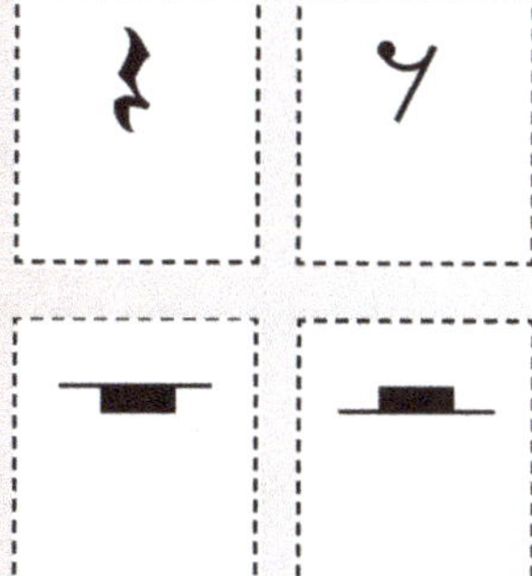

Note A4

Clefi's Little Notebook, pg. 42 and 43

In the **treble clef**, the primary note **A4** sits in the **second space** of the **staff**, like the little robin Adam fluttering between the second and the third lines in *Clefi's Little Notebook* on page 39.

E Practice drawing the **A4 whole**, **half**, **quarter**, and **eighth notes**.

E **Identify** all the **A4** notes in the **song** and **circle** them in **red**. Next, **find** the **C4** notes and **circle** them in **blue**. Lastly, **find** all the **notes** placed on the **staff lines** and **circle** them in **yellow**.

E Write the **order number** for each **note** of the **fourth octave**.

C4	E4	A4	D4	F4	B4	G4
1						

Learn the song "Rain is Falling" from Clefi's Songbook found at the end of *Clefi's Little Notebook* (page 55).

- Mark the **downbeats** with a small **dash** above each **note**.
- Draw bar lines in **front** of every **downbeat note**.
- **Write** the **time signature** in the space at the **beginning** of the **staff**.
- **Complete** the **notes** to accurately **reflect** their **respective values**.

Connect the **clouds** that **belong** together.

Note B4

Clefi's Little Notebook, pg. 44

In the **treble clef**, the primary note **B4** sits on the **third**, the **middle line** of the staff, like the swallow Betty perched on the third power line in *Clefi's Little Notebook* on page 39. The note B4 can have a **stem** placed on **either side** in the **correct direction**. It's the **last note** of the **fourth octave**.

E Practice drawing the **B4 quarter** and **eighth notes** with **stems** in **either direction**.

When linking the **B4 eighth note** with a **lower note** using a **beam**, we draw the **stem** on its **right side**, pointing **upwards**. Conversely, when connecting it to a **higher note**, we place the **stem** on the **left side**, pointing **downwards**.

E Finish the exercise according to the **example** at the beginning of the staff.

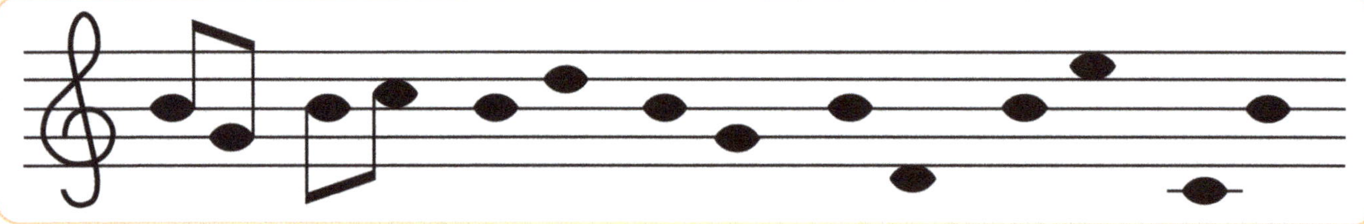

E Write the connected **eighth** notes named below the staff. Then, **look** at the **time signature** and **mark** the **bar lines**.

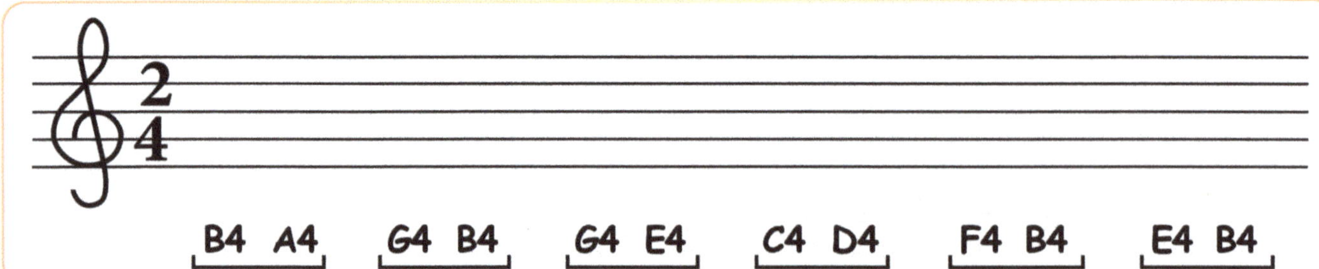

Notes on Lines and in Spaces

Ellen's first and Gaby's second
The middle line is Betty's place
Cousin Daisy loves the fourth one
The fifth one is for Wind's round Face

E   Find the **notes** that **belong** to the **fourth octave** and **circle** them in **green**.

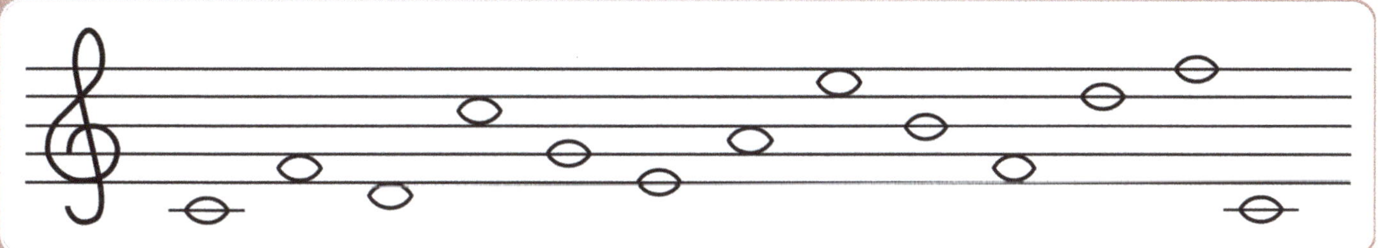

When it's not blowing from
the top line at the swallows
on the lines below, the
wind hides its
F A C E
in the **spaces** of the staff.

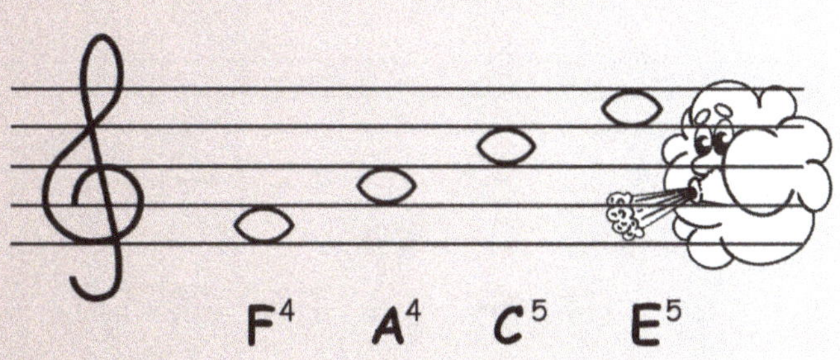

E   Write the **notes** according to the **names** onto the **staff**.

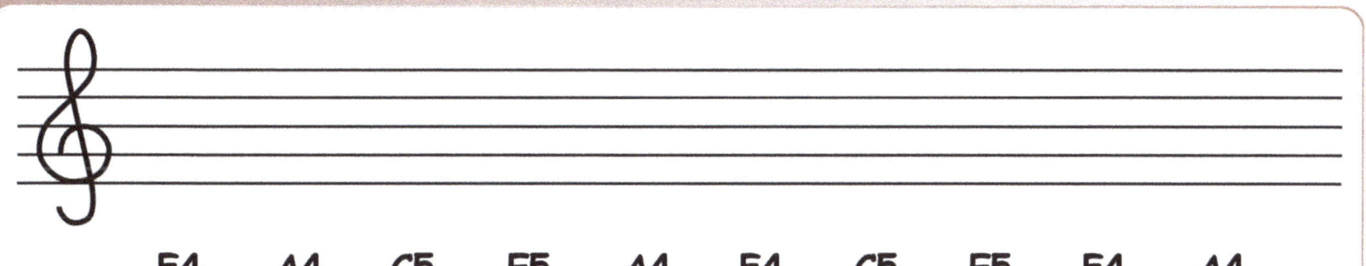

Substitute Musical Staff

We can use one of our **hands** as a **substitute musical staff** and the other one to **show notes** of the song as we sing.

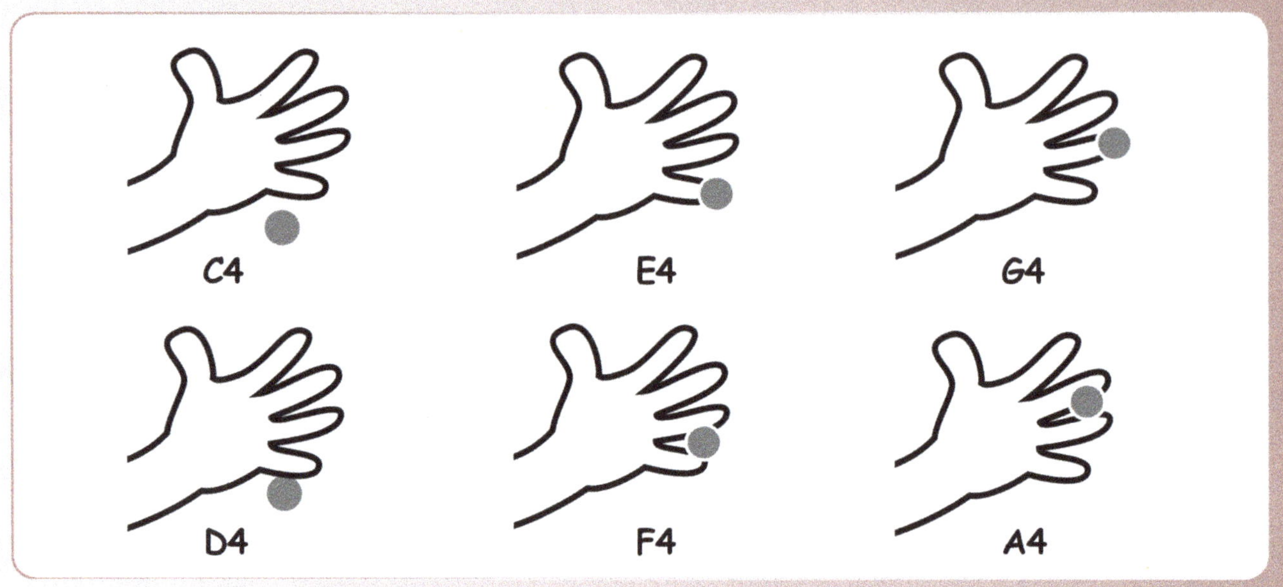

E | **Show** the musical patterns below on your **hand** while **singing** the **names** of the **notes**.

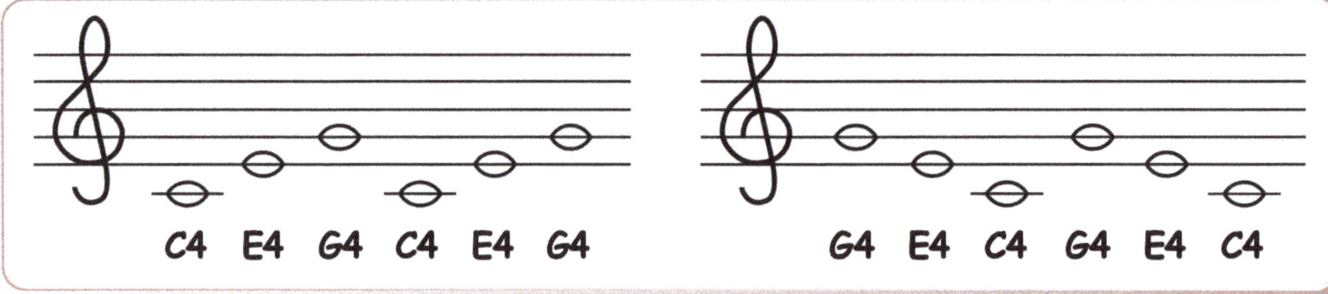

E | The **song** "Little Vixen, Run!" starts with the **tones** we learned **showing** on **our hands**. Adjust the **note values** so they represent the **correct rhythm**. Name all the **notes**.

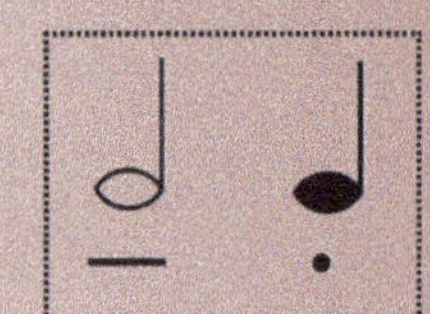

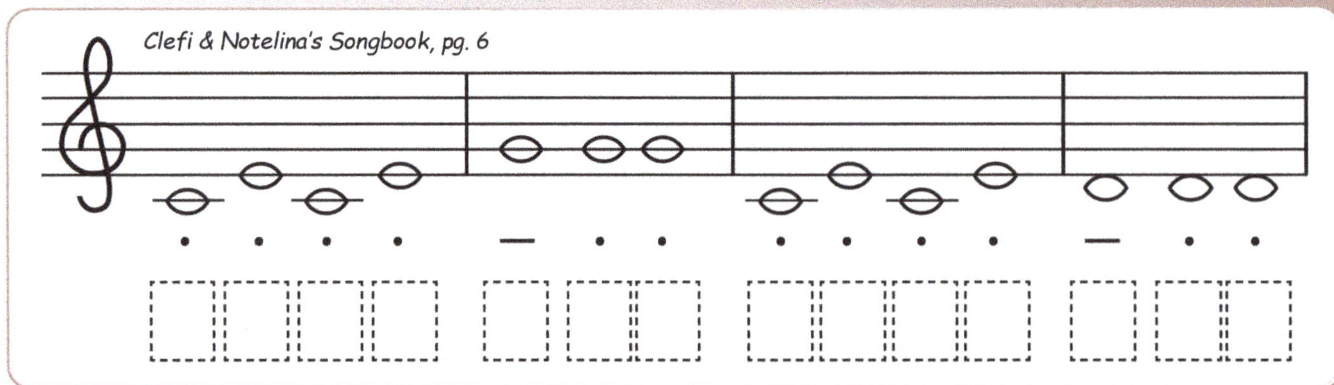

 Learn the song "The Bass Behind Our Stove" from *Clefi's Musical Instruments* (page 30). **Sing** it using the **names** of the **notes**, and **circle** the **notes** on the staff **lines** in **red**.

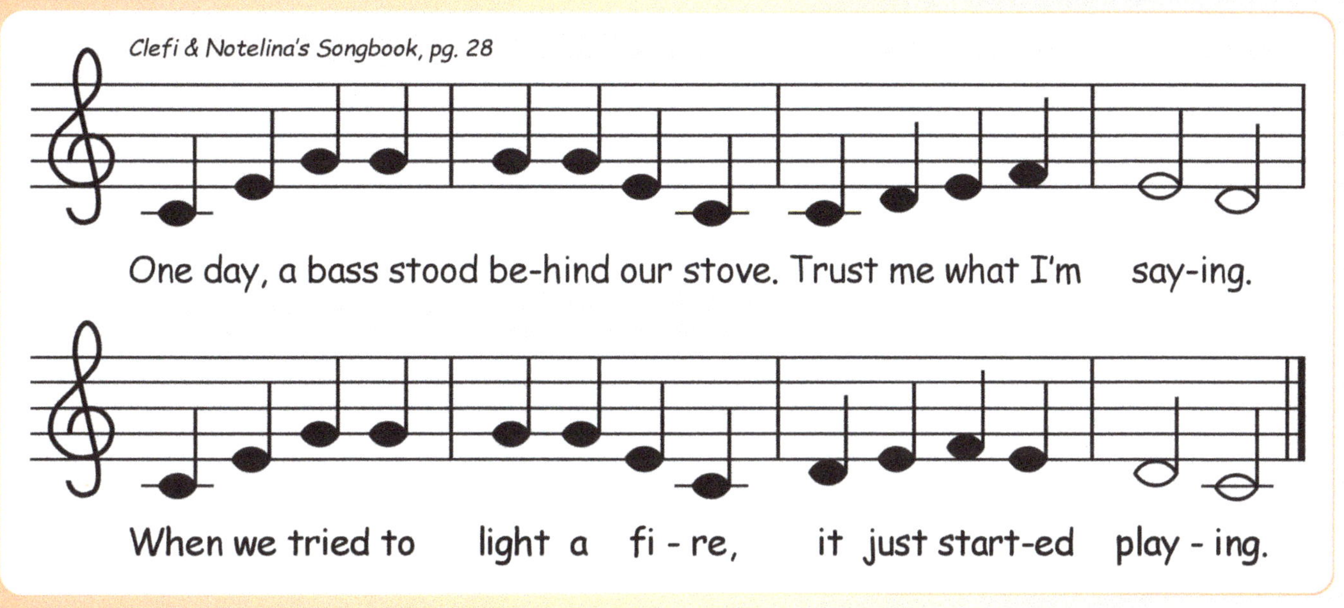

 Copy the measure that contain words **"stove"** and **"saying."**

 Sing the song "Little Vixen, Run!" from *Clefi's Little Notebook* (page 54) using the **names** of the **notes** and **show** them on your **hand**. Then, **circle** the **measures** starting with the note **C4**, all in different colors.

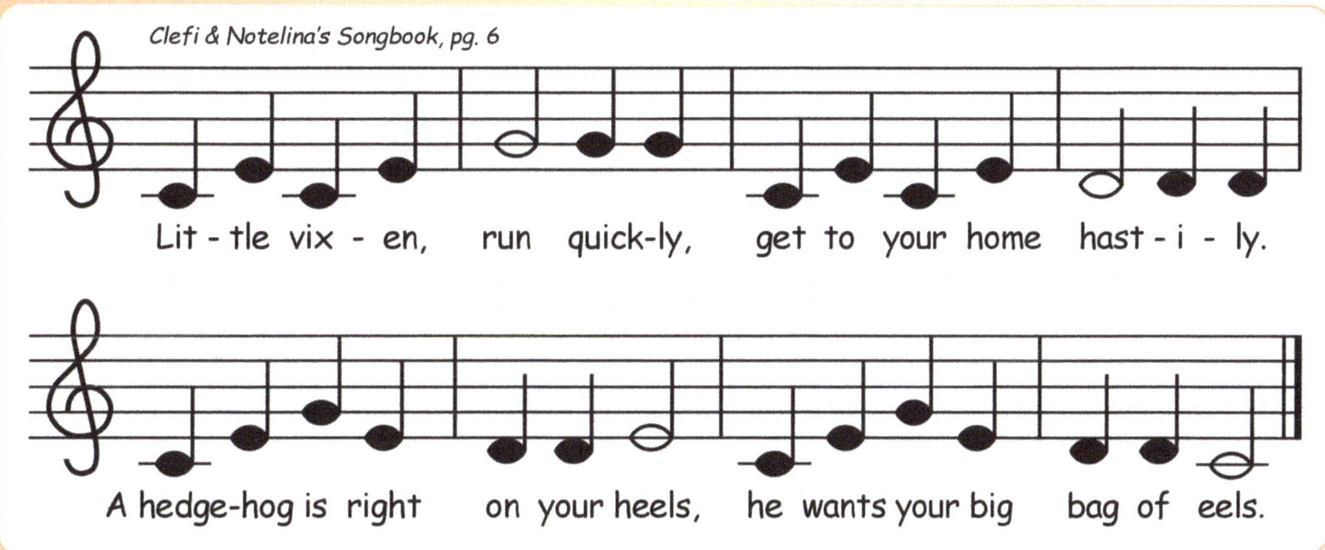

Ascending & Descending Melodies

ASCENDING - RISING MELODY

tones are climbing up

DESCENDING - FALLING MELODY

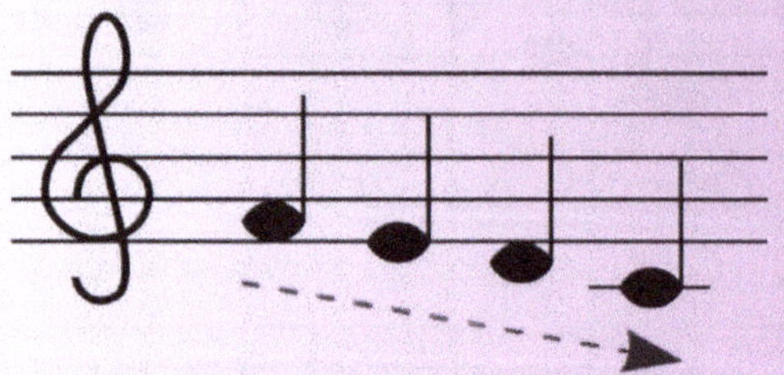

tones are stepping down

E Which of the first two measures of the songs you know starts with an ascending - rising melody? **Color** the **house** with the **ascending melody yellow** and the one with the **descending melody green**.

E Fill in the **notes** with the **correct rhythm. Follow** their **names** and **dots** and **dashes** below the staff. Mark the **rising** and **falling melody** using **arrows**.

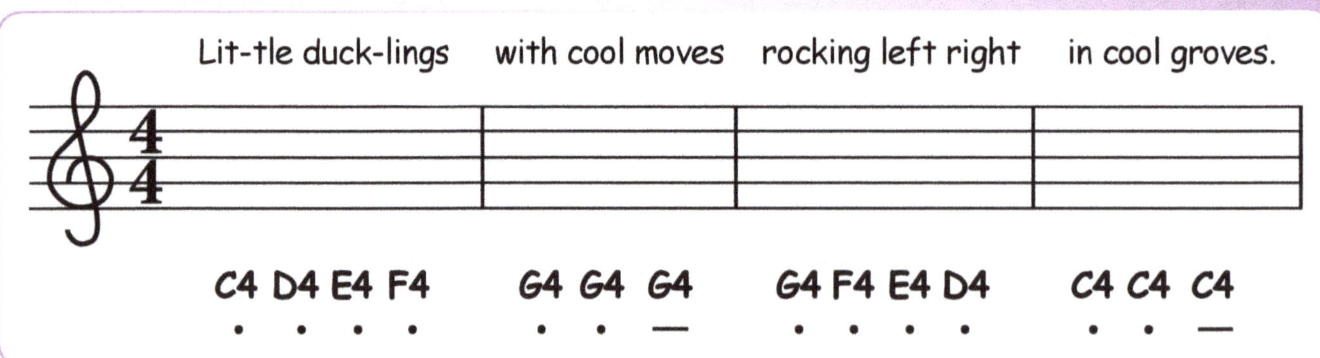

E The **balloons** with the **measures** from the song "Little Vixen Under a Tree" from *Clefi's Musical Instruments* (page 18) **flew away**. Catch them, **number** them in the **correct order**, and **align them** as a **continuous staff**. Then, **fill in the music clef** and the **meter**. Finally, **color** the **balloons** with the **rising melody yellow** and the ones with the **falling melody blue**. **Color** the ones with the **same tones red**.

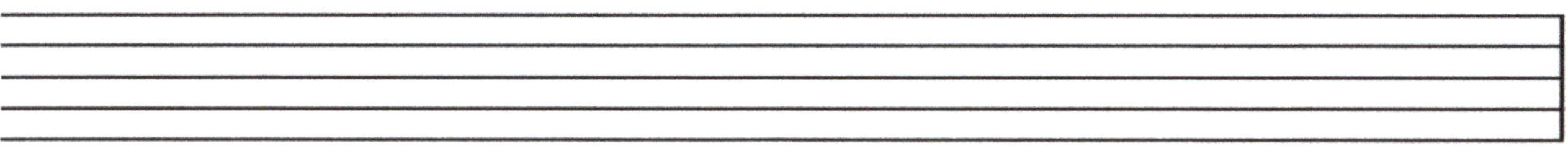

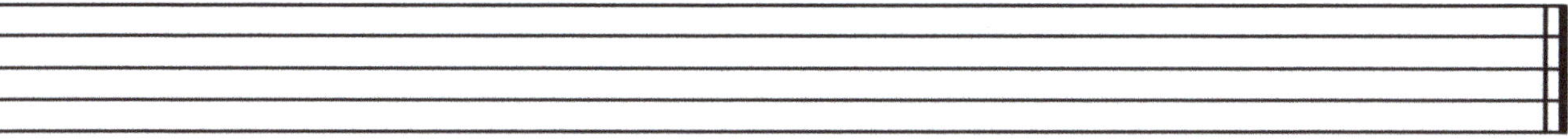

Clefi & Notelina's Songbook, pg. 26

Note C5

Clefi's Little Notebook, pg. 44

To complete the **C major scale** in the fourth octave, we must add the **first** note of the **fifth** octave. The **last note of the C major scale** built from the notes of the **fourth** octave is the note **C5**, which is also the **first note** of the **fifth octave**.

In the treble clef, the note C5 sits in the **third space** of the **staff**.

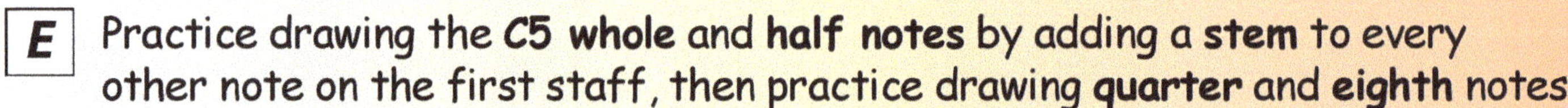

E Practice drawing the **C5 whole** and **half notes** by adding a **stem** to every other note on the first staff, then practice drawing **quarter** and **eighth** notes.

E Practice recognizing **C4** and **C5** notes.
- **Name** all the **notes** on the staff.
- **Circle** all notes **C5** red.

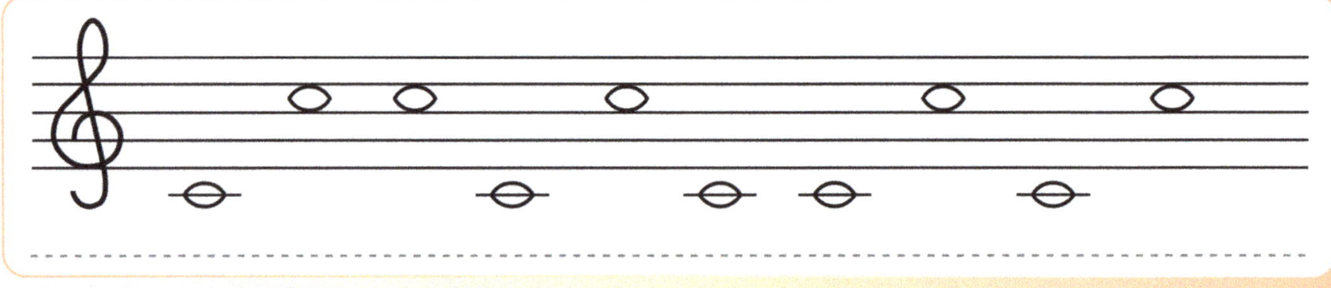

E Write **half notes** according to their names. Mind the **stem placement!**

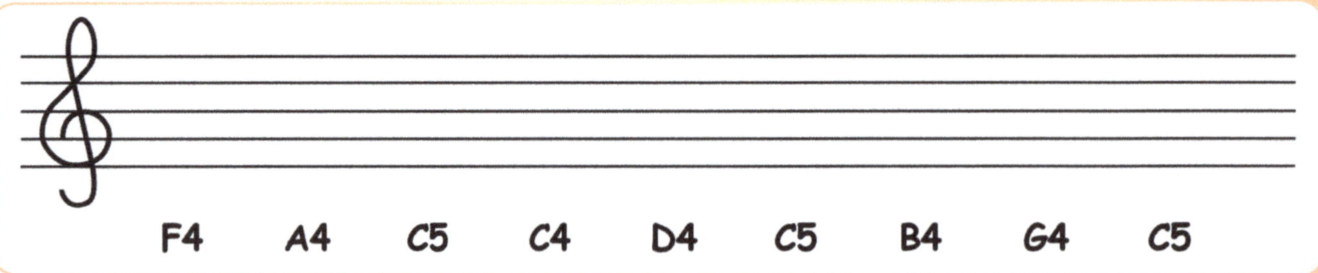

Sing "I'm Not Going to the Forest" **using** the **names** of the **notes**. Circle all the notes **C5**. Try to come up with your own **lyrics** and **name** the song.

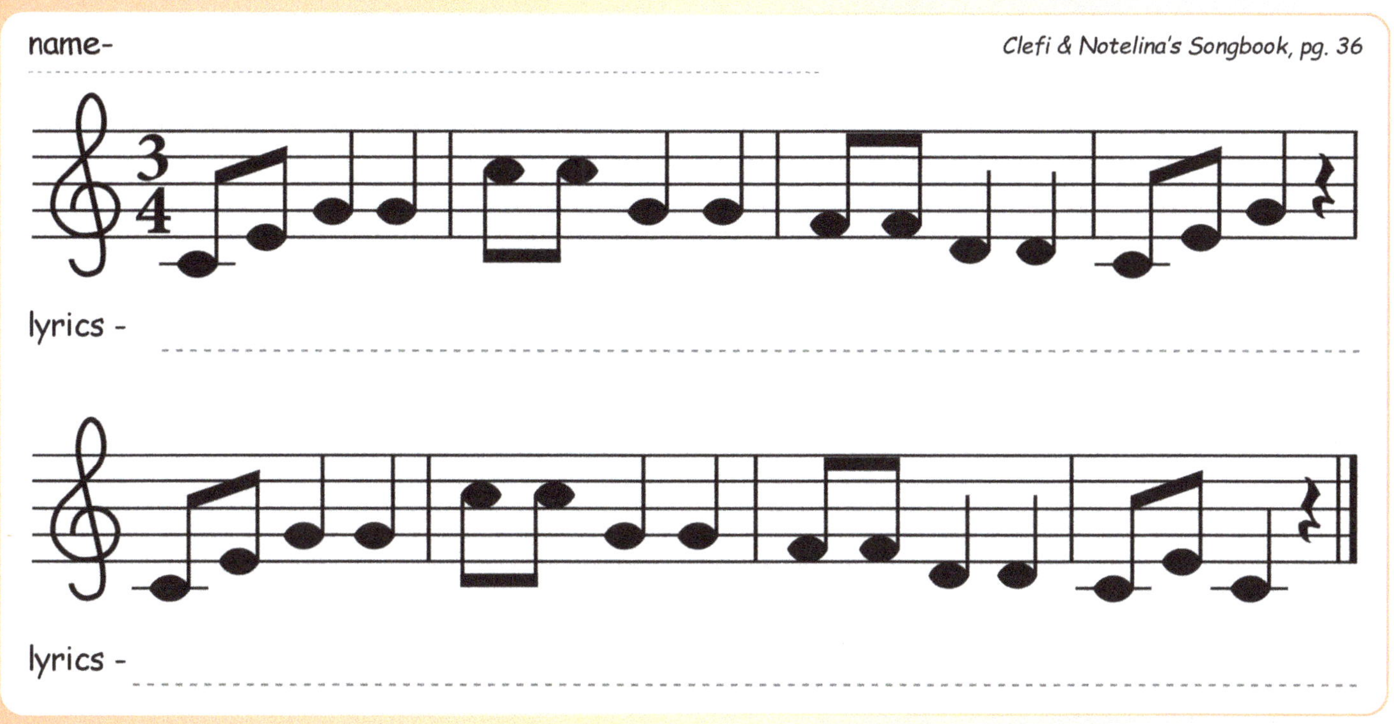

Fill in the **notes** in the correct **rhythm**, then sing the song using the **name of the notes.**, and do not forget to learn the actual song!

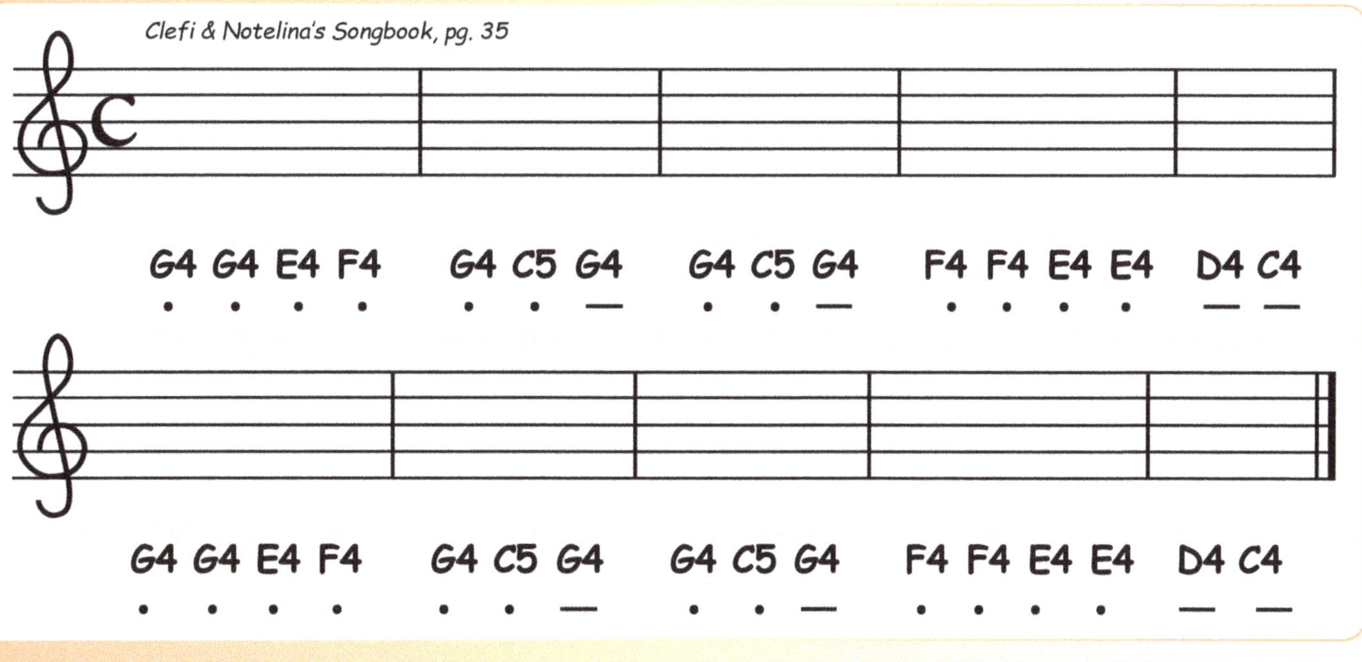

Copy the **measure** with the note **C5**.

How many times did the **measure appear** in the song?

Notes Review

E Draw a **treble** clef and the **whole** notes according to their **names**.

C4 D4 E4 F4 G4 A4 B4 C5 D4 G4

E Draw a **treble** clef and the **eighth** notes according to their **names**. Connect the **underlined notes** with a **beam**.

A4 C5 <u>D4 E4</u> B4 C4 C5 <u>F4 G4</u> A4 <u>C4 E4</u>

E Sing the song "Little Turtle Dove" from Clefi's Songbook at the end of *Clefi's Little Notebook* on page 60. Write the **names** of the **notes** on the dotted lines below the staff. **Circle** all notes **C5** in red and all notes **C4** in green.

Clefi & Notelina's Songbook, pg. 18

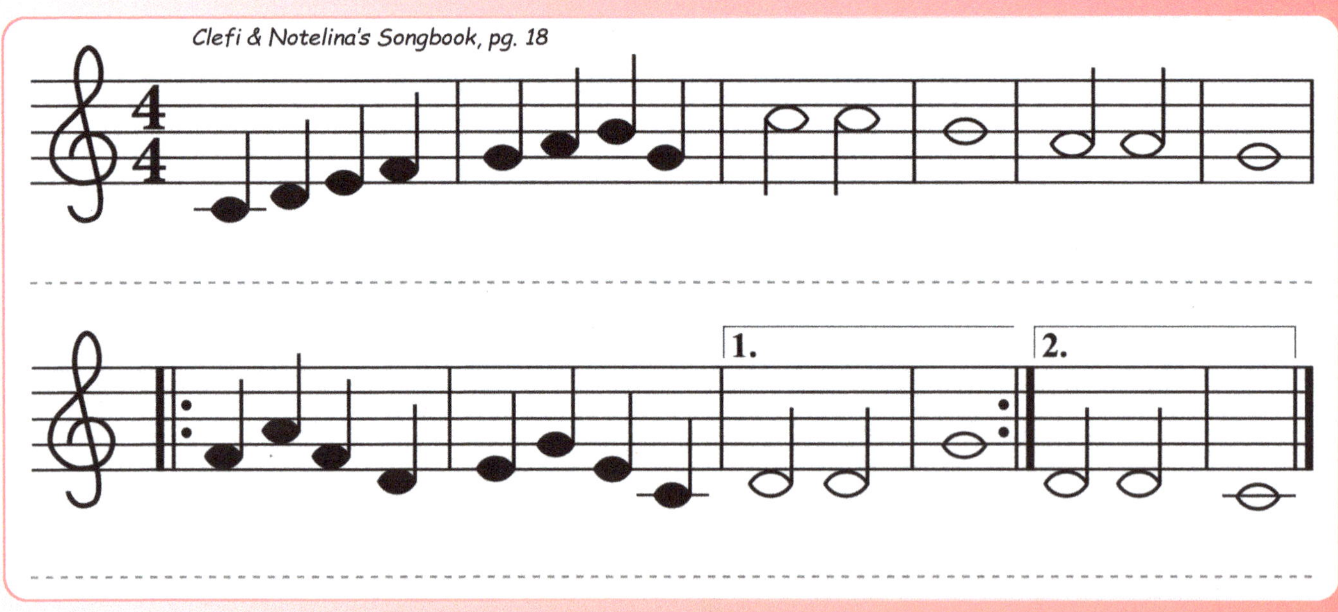

Major Fifth Chord

Clefi's Music Notebook 1, pg. 17

Like the song on page 25, the following beautiful Czech folk song "A little Pear Tree" starts with the **melodic major fifth chord**. The **fifth chord** is built from a scale's **first**, **third**, and **fifth** degrees. The chord is **major** if the **scale** is in a **major, happy** mode. This song presents the chord as a **melody**, with the notes **following** each other in a **melodic pattern**.
That's why we call it the **melodic major fifth chord**.

E Sing the song using the **names** of the **notes**, then **copy** the **measures** with this **rhythm**:

E Copy the **first three notes** of the song. Do you know **other songs** that start with the **same melodic pattern**, the **melodic major fifth chord**?

E How **many times** does the note **C5** appear in the song?

Fifth Octave

Clefi's Music Notebook 1, pg. 4

The note **C5** marks the **beginning** of the **fifth** octave. This octave includes the tones from the **primary tone row** as in the fourth, the middle octave, but each is **raised an octave higher**. When **notating the** fifth octave on the staff, the notes are arranged in the **same sequence** as they appear on the **keyboard, alternating** between **spaces** and **lines.** This time, we will utilize **several ledger lines above the staff** to complete the tone row.

Just as the notes of the **fourth** octave are labeled with the number **4** following the letter, the notes of the **fifth** octave carry the number **5.**

E Fill in the **full names** of all the **notes** on the keyboard.

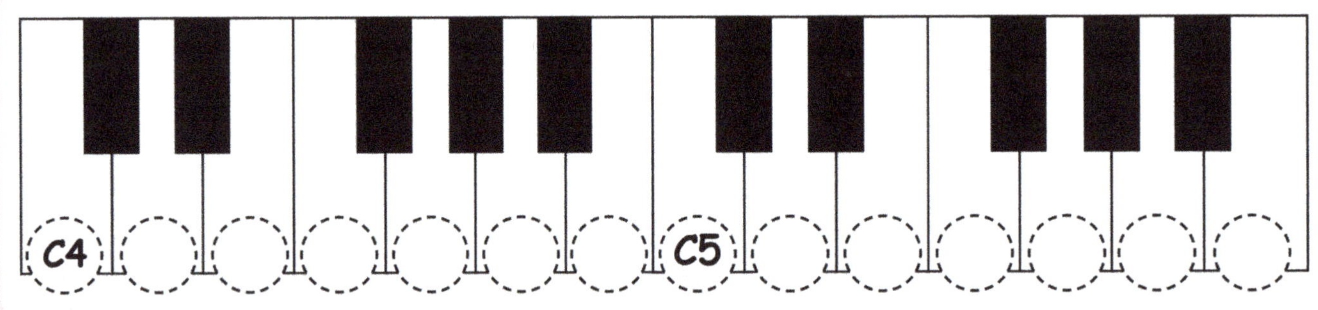

E Add the **stems** to the notes. Circle the notes **C5** and **E5** in **red.** You know them from page 19, where we talked about the notes in spaces - **F A C E.**

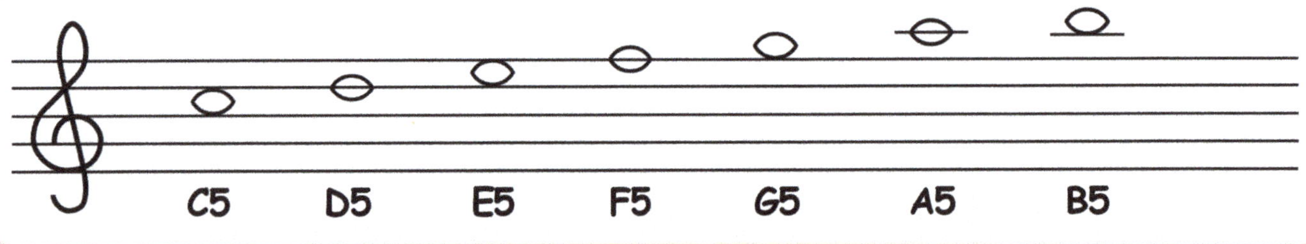

E Write **quarter** notes according to the names below the staff. Can you identify the octave to which these notes belong?

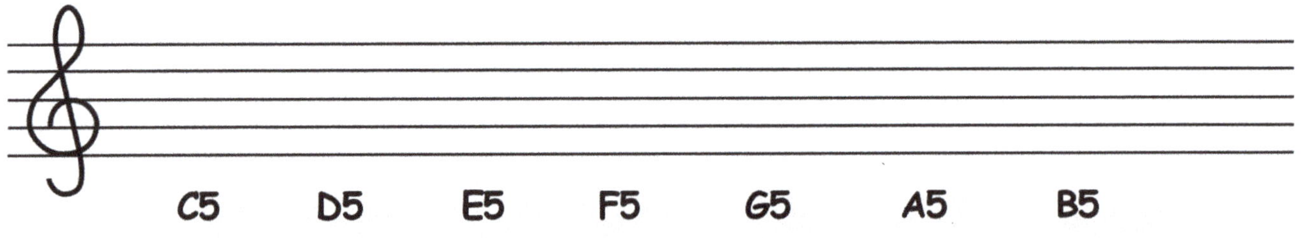

E Look at the notation of the song "Little Vixen Under a Tree" in the **fifth** octave. **Name** all the **notes** on the dotted line below the staff.

E Write the **whole notes** according to the **names** below the staff.

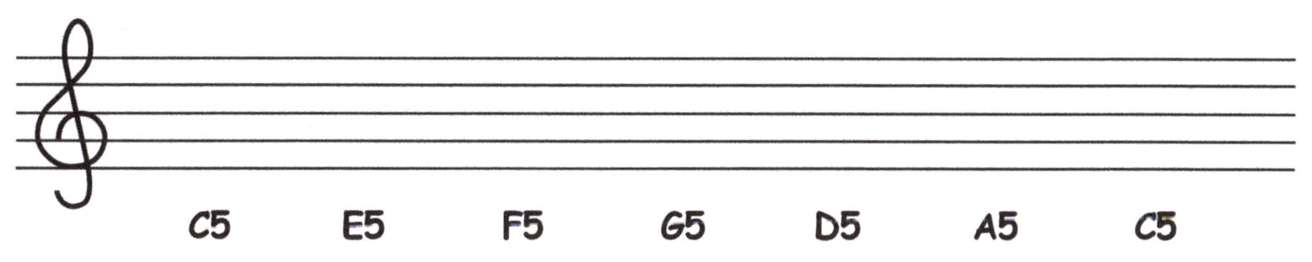

E **Write** the parts of the songs you know (to the left), but this time in the **fifth octave. Name** all the notes. We call this the **octave transposition.**

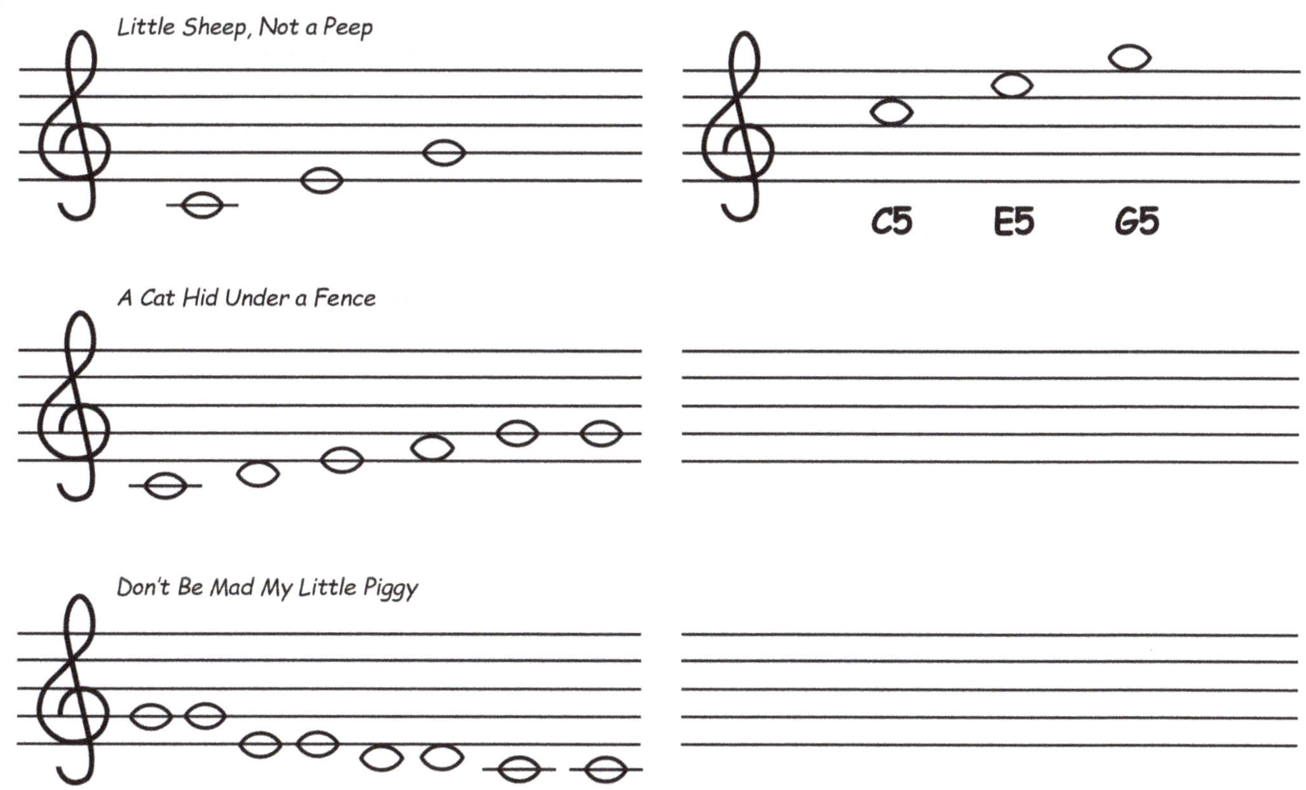

Third Octave

Clefi's Music Notebook 1, pg. 4

Same as we can go from the fourth octave up, we can go down and meet the notes of the third octave. We will repeat the tones of the primary tone row, but this time in reverse order.

Just as the notes of the **fourth octave** are labeled with the number **4**
and those of the **fifth octave** carry the number **5,**
the notes of the **third octave** are labeled with the number **3.**

E First, starting from note **C4,** fill in the **notes** of the **fourth,** the **middle** octave. Next, fill in the **notes** of the **third** octave in **reverse** order. Start from **B3 and** continue to the **left** or **downward.**

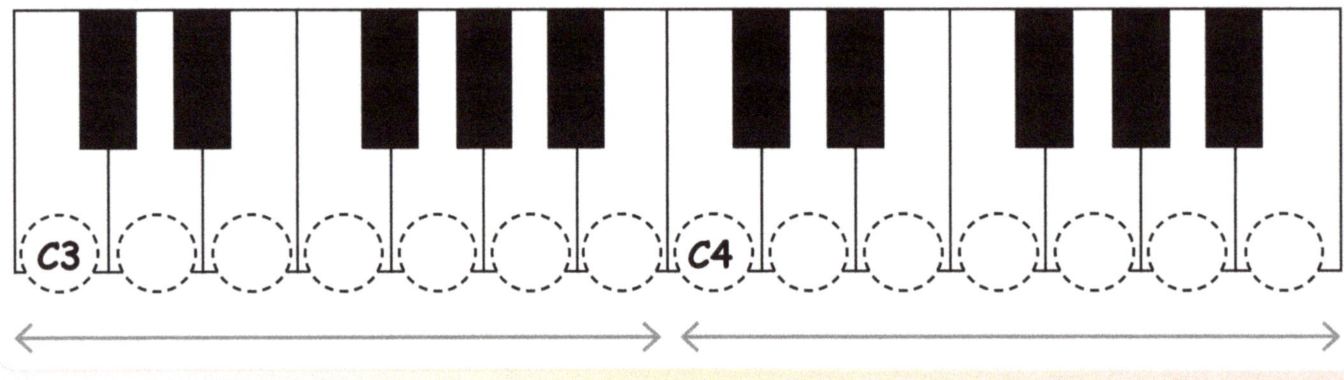

In the **treble clef,** it's easiest to read the **notes** of the **third octave** from the **C4** down. The lower ones need a lot of **ledger lines.** It's much easier to notate them in the **bass clef.** Since we can use up to **five ledger lines,** it is good to know how to write and read the notes of the third octave in the treble clef, too.

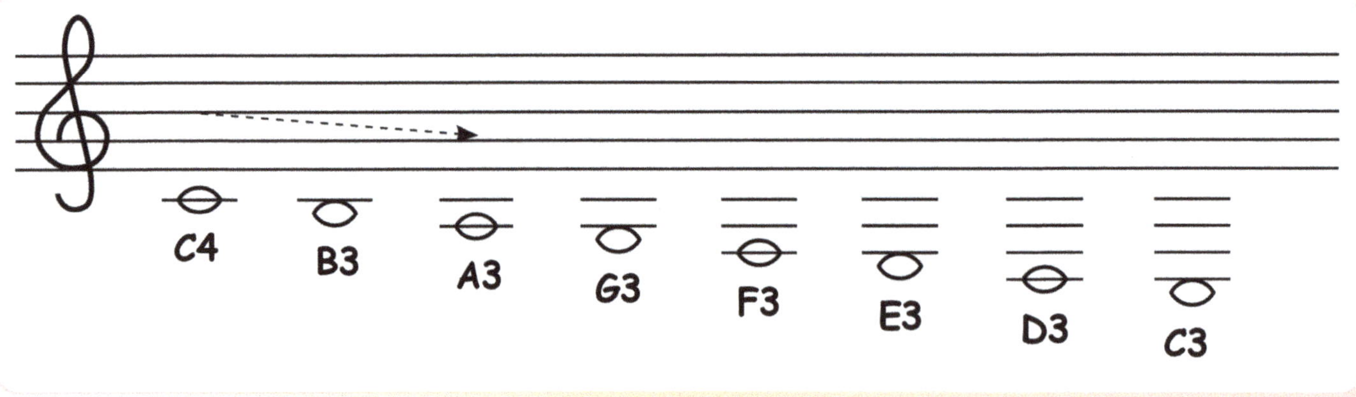

E Write the notes
C4, B3, A3, and G3.

E Practice writing the notes of the **third octave** in the **treble clef** by writing the beginning of the song "Go to Sleep, My Little Starlight."

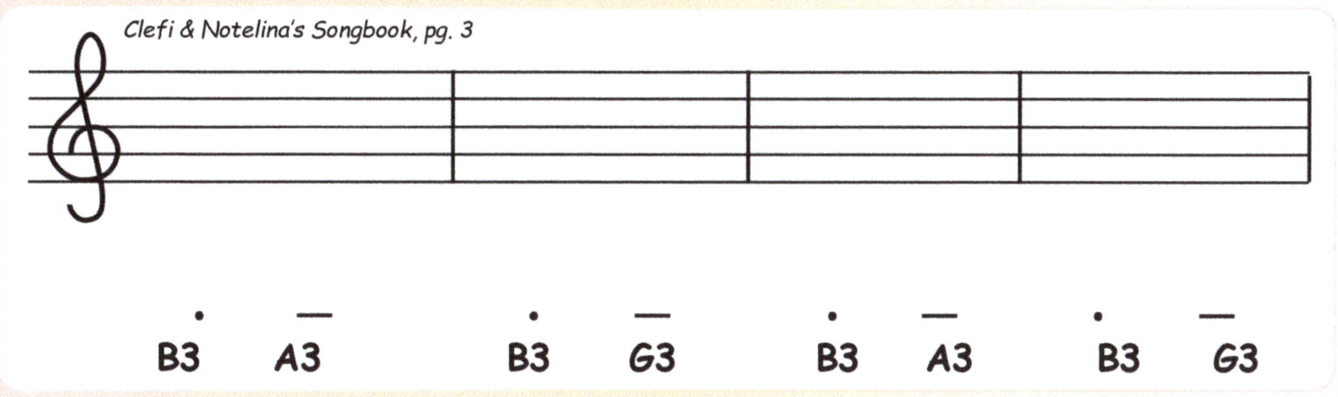

E Can you read all these notes? Write down their names.

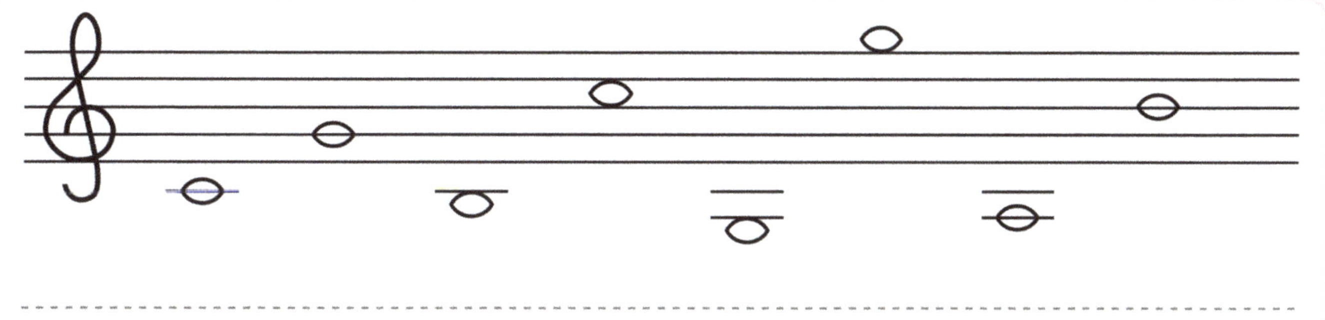

E Color the balloons with the notes of the **4th octave yellow**, the ones from the **3rd octave blue**, and the notes of the **5th octave red**.

Final Review

E   **Name** all the **notes**, **sing** them, and **show** them using your **"hand staff."**

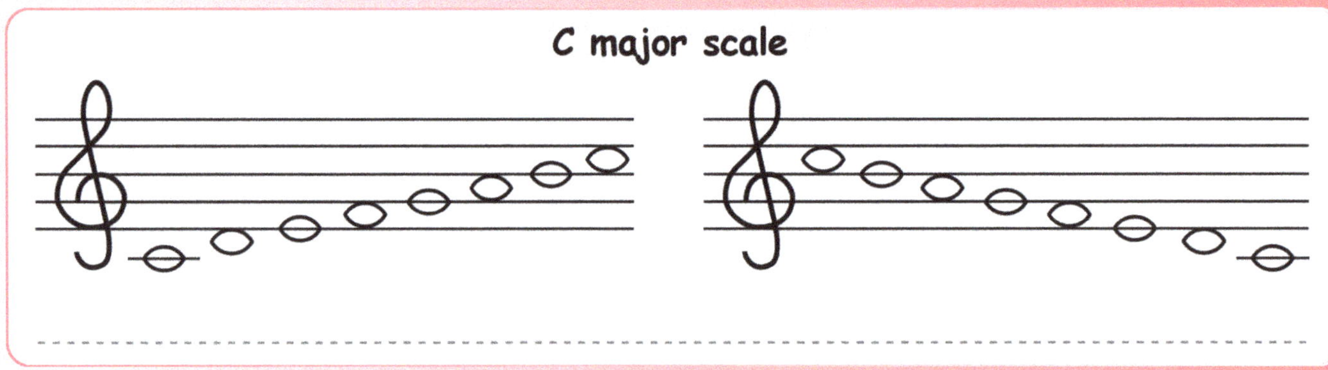

E   Learn and sing the song "Run, Run, Run, Katy!" from *Celfi's Little Notebook* (page 57). **Name** all the **notes**, complete them according to the **meter** and the **dots** and **dashes** (mind the placement of the **stems!**), and **circle** those in the **fifth octave**.

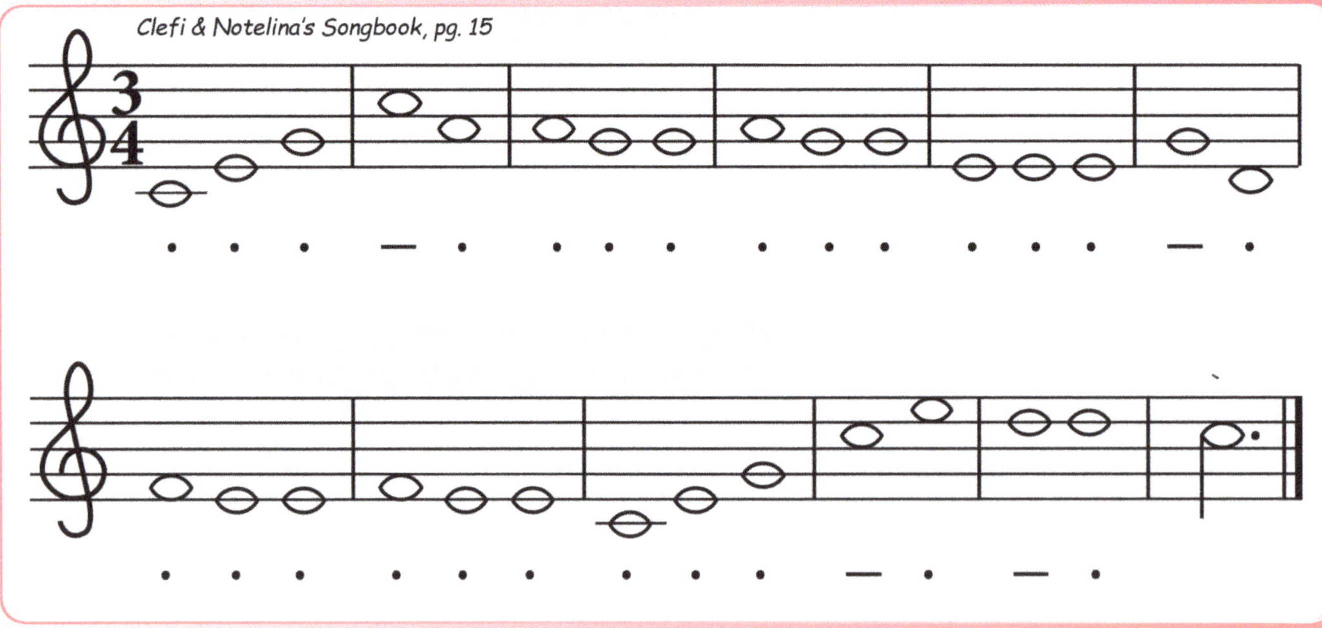

CERTIFICATE

OF COMPLETION

This certificate is presented to:

____

For successfully completing

Clefi's Music Workbook 2

____

music education teacher

Clefi's Little American-British Music Dictionary

Note & Rest Values

Whole note .... Semibreve

Whole rest .... Semibreve pause

Half note .... Minim

Half rest .... Minim pause

Quarter note .... Crotchet

Quarter rest .... Crotchet pause

Eighth note .... Quaver

Eight rest .... Quaver pause

Note Distances

Whole step .... Tone

Half step .... Semitone

Octaves

Fourth octave .... One-line octave

Fifth octave .... Two-line octave

Notes

C4-B4 .... c'-b' (one-line c-b)

C5 .... c" (two-line c)

Join Clefi's musical family!
Clefi invites you to visit his dedicated webpage and explore the enchanting musical world of Dr. Eva's New Music Education School Series. Learn more about the author and about the content of every volume of the series, dive into engaging materials, find answers to all the exercises, discover more songs, and further deepen your love and understanding of music and music education. Come make music with us!

www.bumblebeenotes.com/clefis-musical-world

www.bumblebeenotes.com/music-publishing

www.ingramcontent.com/pod-product-compliance
Lightning Source LLC
Chambersburg PA
CBHW040220110726
48005CB00019B/3091